Numerology

by Lauren David Peden

THE MYSTICAL ARTS

Illustrations by Jenny Tylden Wright

WARNER ⦿ TREASURES

PUBLISHED BY WARNER BOOKS

A TIME WARNER COMPANY

Warner Treasures is a
trademark of Warner Books, Inc.

Warner Books, Inc.,
1271 Avenue of the Americas,
New York, NY 10020

 A Time Warner Company

Printed in China
First Printing: March 1996
10 9 8 7 6 5 4 3 2 1

ISBN: 0-446-91012-0

Numerology

THE MYSTICAL ARTS

INTRODUCTION

Numbers play an important role in our everyday lives, ranging from the mundane—telephone numbers, zip codes, height—to the meaningful—birthdays, anniversaries, weight. Nowhere is the meaning of numbers more prevalent than in the science of numerology.

This ancient arithmetic system helps explain who we are, where we're going in life, and how we can best achieve our goals. As with astrology or palmistry, we can use numerology to help us make the most of our talents and to help us fulfill our promise. When you explore the world of numerology, you explore your inner self and the world around you, as well. So come on along—it promises to be a fascinating, memorable, and life-enhancing journey!

Add It Up

Numerology is easy to learn, because it involves only simple addition. Just keep reducing double-digit numbers until you have arrived at a single-digit number between 1 and 9. For example, 7 + 9 = 16, which is further reduced by adding 1 + 6, which would leave you with 7. Likewise, 1996 would reduce to 7 (1 + 9 + 9 + 6 = 25, and 2 + 5 = 7).

DESTINY AND BIRTHDATE NUMBERS

The Destiny and Birthdate Numbers, which reveal your personality and general outlook, are based on your date of birth. The Destiny Number is thought to be the most significant and influential number we deal with in numerology, since it can never be changed or altered. It represents what we are meant to learn during our lifetime—our raison d'être, if you will. To figure out your Destiny Number, add up all the numbers in your date of birth (day, month, and year). As an example, we'll use September 13, 1934. As September is the ninth month, that yields 9 + 1 + 3 + 1 + 9 + 3 + 4, which totals 30. We further reduce 30 (3 + 0) to get a Destiny Number of 3. The only double digits left intact when the Destiny Number is computed are 11 and 22, which are considered Master Numbers in numerology. The Master Numbers are thought to have higher vibrations than their single-digit counterparts. People with these numbers possess unique leadership characteristics; they have the innate ability to inspire other people and to be of service to humankind. These numbers are also indicative of extraordinary powers of spiritual and intellectual perception.

In addition to the Destiny Number, our Birthdate Number also gives us invaluable information about our personal characteristics. This number represents the intrinsic qualities that make each of us unique as individuals. To calculate your Birthdate Number, add the numbers of the day of the month on which you were born. If you were born on the 28th of the month, for example, your Birthdate Number is 1 (2 + 8 = 10; 1 + 0 = 1). If you were born on the 9th, you're a 9, and if you were born on the 14th, you're a 5 (1 + 4 = 5). NOTE: If you were born on the 11th or 22nd of the month (or if your Birthdate Number reduces to 11 or 22), keep adding until you have a single-digit number. The Birthdate Number is not governed by the Master Numbers. Once you have figured out your Destiny and Birthdate Numbers, look up their meanings on the following pages.

ONE

DESTINY NUMBER: A person whose Destiny Number is one is meant to learn about independence and individuality. In order to get the most out of life, ones need to concentrate on enhancing their determination, motivation, creativity, self-confidence, and leadership abilities. Ones will not succeed if they follow the crowd or allow themselves to become overly dependent on other people. Only by being totally self-reliant can they fulfill their destiny. In addition to learning how to promote their good qualities, ones also need to learn to squelch their natural tendency to be bossy, selfish, and egotistical. When fully developed, a Number One Destiny offers boundless opportunity for personal growth and self-fulfillment.

BIRTHDATE: People born on the 1st, 10th, 19th, or 28th of the month are ones. They possess great planning and organizational skills, and are ruled by their head rather than their heart. They are admirably forthright in their dealings with others and have no trouble expressing their opinions. Although ones enjoy being in the company of other people, they are loners by nature. They are idealistic, independent, original thinkers who feel extremely comfortable in positions of leadership. In fact, ones don't like being in second-place positions of any kind.

TWO

DESTINY NUMBER: A person with a Destiny Number of two must learn to be cooperative, peaceful, considerate, and humble. In order to feel fulfilled, twos need to develop and enhance their sensitivity, diplomacy, kindness, and patience. Number twos do best when they put other people first, as it is their destiny to be of service to others. They tend to form strong bonds with other people, and are completely dependent on their friendships and/or love relationships for personal fulfillment. Twos do not respond well to aggressiveness or fast-paced situations; they are most comfortable when things progress slowly and steadily. In fact, they flourish in the type of secure environment that others might find oppressive. Twos must learn not to be too moody, sensitive, impressionable, or indecisive. A fully developed Number Two Destiny promotes a wonderful sense of love, harmony, and companionship.

BIRTHDATE: Those born on the 2nd, 11th, 20th, and 29th are twos. They are gentle, com-

passionate, romantic souls who are
driven by their desire to help others and to promote a peaceful, harmonious atmosphere. Twos
are open, intuitive, and receptive to other people. They are born followers, and usually don't
do well in positions of authority. They are
innately creative, however, which makes them

especially well suited for any type of artistic career. Twos tend to marry for life, and prefer to be surrounded by people rather than spend time alone. These homebodies truly appreciate life's creature comforts, including aesthetic pleasures such as gourmet meals and fine wine.

THREE
DESTINY NUMBER:

The person with Destiny Number three should strive to be cheerful, imaginative, optimistic, creative, and sociable. Threes must learn to enjoy everything that life has to offer and to develop their innate sense of charm and wit. In order to feel content and live up to their potential, threes need to live for the moment. Threes are the life of the party. They're vivacious, high-spirited people who love to have a good time, and they aren't happy unless everyone else is having a good time, too. In fact, anxiety, worry, and cynicism cause outgoing threes immeasurable discomfort, so they don't often give in to these unpleasant emotions. Threes are extremely articulate and express themselves with ease (they are also adept at making others feel comfortable). Threes tend to be late bloomers, and may be somewhat serious when they're young. In fact, their main purpose in life is to learn to overcome any egotistical, pessimistic, excessively responsible, or antisocial tendencies they may have. A fully developed Number Three Destiny provides a glorious opportunity for a carefree, interesting, and charmed lifestyle.

BIRTHDATE:

People born on the 3rd,
12th, 21st, or 30th are threes.
They are gregarious, outgoing, and usually

very popular among their peers. Expressive, communicative threes are born leaders who thrive in the spotlight. They're ambitious by nature and don't shy away from hard work; in fact, threes' dogged determination guarantees that they'll succeed in any endeavor. Fun-loving threes are extremely fashion-conscious. They adore children and animals, and usually have several of each. Their optimistic, sunny disposition allows them to see the bright side of any situation, and they aren't given to brooding or sarcasm, even if it's warranted.

FOUR

DESTINY NUMBER: A person with a Destiny Number of four must learn to be practical, serious, honest, and self-disciplined. Fours need to develop industrious determination in order to fulfill their promise and to gain emotional and financial security. At their best, fours are dependable and trustworthy, hard workers who do whatever it takes to get the job done. All of their accomplishments are the direct result of careful planning and deliberate, conscientious effort. When it comes to love and friendship, they gravitate toward solid, dependable, like-minded people (the saying "A friend in need is a friend indeed" was probably coined by a four). Because of their natural workhorse tendencies, fours must take care not to become rigid, dull, or hypercritical. Change can be *fun*, four. As long as they know their strengths (and limits), and are willing to invest the necessary time and effort, fours can achieve even their loftiest goals. Patience is the key to their success.

BIRTHDATE: People born on the 4th, 13th,

22nd, and 31st are fours. These people are propelled by an innate sense of duty and purpose, and they possess an extremely strong work ethic. They are linear, focused thinkers who excel in mechanical or mathematical jobs. Fours don't like to waste time, and are happier at work than at play. They tend to be rather cautious and deliberate. In fact, fours pride themselves on being different from other people; as a result, they attract friends and lovers from unusual backgrounds. Although fours are trustworthy and dependable when it comes to relationships, they tend to be somewhat moody, and their feelings may be easily hurt.

FIVE

DESTINY NUMBER: A person whose Destiny Number is five needs to develop enthusiasm, curiosity, cleverness, and verbal expressiveness. The life of fives revolves around constant change, so they should strive to be flexible, versatile, broad-minded, and adventurous if they are to live up to their inherent potential. Emotionally and physically, fives are like sharks: If they don't move, they'll die. They thrive on new experiences and are happiest when they're meeting new people, traveling to exotic locales, or eating unusual foods. Fives' transient inclinations are not easily tempered, and if they should attempt to knuckle down by taking on a nine-to-five job or by trying to force themselves to conform to a traditional relationship, they'll only succeed in making themselves miserable. Because of their innate flightiness, fives have to concentrate on not being indifferent, too impulsive, or self-indulgent. A well-developed five is able to revel in life's bounty.

BIRTHDATE: People born on the 5th, 14th, or 23rd of the month are fives. They are highly adaptable, sociable creatures who make friends easily. They prize freedom, travel, and change of any kind. They're always on the go and don't mind living out of a suitcase. Fives feel hemmed in by traditional nine-to-five jobs or traditional long-term marriages. They shun physical labor and excel in professions that allow them to utilize their impressive intellectual acumen. They are natural risk takers who work best under pressure and thrive on stress. When it comes to love, fives' credo is "The more the merrier." They favor serial monogamy over infidelity, but it's hard to keep

their
interest for any
length of time. Once you've kissed a five, be
prepared to say good-bye.

SIX

DESTINY NUMBER: The person with a Destiny Number of six should work on enhancing a sense of responsibility, creativity, and selflessness. Sixes need to develop dependable, loving relationships and must strive to be as giving, friendly, and affectionate as possible. A highly evolved number six is an early bloomer who prizes stable domesticity above all else; these are the people who marry for love and stay married for life. Sixes are most content when they embrace their duties and make themselves useful. They tend to form deep, lasting friendships and have strong ties to their community. Sixes are wise "old souls," and while they like a good time as much as the next person, they are never childish or self-indulgent (although they can be too trusting of other people, which sometimes results in disappointment). Sixes can also be somewhat indecisive and irresponsible, and they must learn to overcome this tendency (along with their overprotective, stubborn streak). At their best, sixes are idealistic, loving, and dependable do-gooders who brighten the lives of the people around them.

BIRTHDATE: Those born on the 6th, 15th, or 24th of the month are sixes. They are responsible, supportive, considerate people who tend to be mature for their age. They appreciate art, aesthetic beauty, and the finer things in life. Sixes also prize domestic harmony, and they excel at creating a cozy, comfortable home environment. In social situations, sixes use their intuitive powers of perception and their caring, vivacious personality to draw out other people and put them at ease. Sixes themselves need to feel loved and appreciated, and they have a well-developed sense of right and wrong. Because of this, they

tend to settle happily into care-giving positions at home or at work.

SEVEN

DESTINY NUMBER: A Destiny Number of seven indicates that the person's overall goal in life is to work on enhancing spiritual, analytical, intuitive, and independent characteristics. They need to develop their wisdom and intellect and should not shy away from solitary pursuits. Sevens are mature, introspective thinkers with philosophical leanings, and they blossom only by nurturing their innate intellectual capacity. In fact, sevens are happiest when they are trying to solve a problem or are rooting around to get to the bottom of things (and they won't give

up until they find what they're looking for). The hustle and bustle of the traditional nine-to-five business world is anathema to slow, deliberate sevens. In relationships, sevens are unusually steadfast and stable. They are inherently trustworthy, honorable people, and expect the same from their friends and lovers. Sevens must learn to temper their tendency to be uncompromising perfectionists. At their best, sevens are open-minded, analytical thinkers who love to ponder life's great mysteries and to take pleasure in sharing their findings with others.

BIRTHDATE: People born on the 7th, 16th, or 25th of the month are sevens. For the most part, sevens are quiet, reserved, introspective people who enjoy sitting around

thinking deep
thoughts. Although
they love to engage in intellectually stimulating discussions, independent sevens are not
outgoing people-pleasers by nature, and

they're most comfortable alone. Because of their intrinsic need for solitude and their emotional aloofness, sevens usually don't have very many close friends, and it's not uncommon for them to remain single for life. Cerebral sevens observe every situation carefully before entering into the fray. They are intuitive, analytical, well-read truth seekers who love to travel. In fact, anything that broadens the mind appeals to knowledge-hungry seven.

EIGHT

DESTINY NUMBER: A person with Destiny Number eight should strive to develop determination, leadership abilities, and business acumen. Eights need to learn not to be afraid to plan big and work hard to make their dreams a reality. If they put their

mind to it and persevere, eights have the Midas touch and can easily accomplish anything they set out to do (this is especially true when it comes to commercial or financial dealings). These farsighted straight-shooters have the ability to inspire and guide other people. Eights are best in the role of high-minded, benevolent boss—they should think big, act decisively, and surround themselves with trustworthy people who will carry out their plans. Efficient, nose-to-the-grindstone eights do best in relationships with like-minded spouses who appreciate their workaholic tendencies (or with significant others who don't mind tending hearth and home while eight brings home the bacon). On the downside, eights must take care not to become power-hungry, money-grubbing schemers. A well-balanced

Number Eight Destiny offers an unmitigated opportunity for financial and material security and for personal fulfillment through dedicated hard work.

BIRTHDATE: People born on the 8th, 17th, or 26th of the month are eights. They are philosophical, serious-minded, dignified individuals who seem older than they really are. Naturally ambitious eights thrive on hard work, and they'll gladly make personal sacrifices if it will further their career or financial interests. (In fact, part of eights' successful striving has to do with an innate fear of being poor, so they always work extra hard to make sure there's money in the bank and food on the table.) They are traditionalists by nature and gravitate toward conventional careers and conven-

tional relationships. Unusual or unstable lifestyles make eights uneasy; they're perfectly happy working a nine-to-five job and commuting home to their spouse and 2.5 kids in the suburbs.

NINE

DESTINY NUMBER: A Destiny Number of nine indicates that the individual needs to hone inspirational, artistic, and selfless characteristics. Nines should strive to be of service to other people, and will best fulfill their destiny by enhancing and promoting their altruistic, philanthropic tendencies. Nines may have to work at being open-minded, but if they are able to approach life (and other people) in a nonjudgmental way, they'll find it personally, emotionally, and even financially rewarding. In fact, well-meaning nines may

find it particularly ironic that their economic situation improves in direct relation to their charitable actions (it seems that the more they do and the less they expect, the more they get in return). Nines usually gravitate toward humanitarian professions such as medicine and law, or toward artistic careers that allow them to nuture other people while they nurture their own creativity. When it comes to friends and lovers, nines are instinctively drawn to older or needy people, and they're not content unless they feel that they're helping others. They must squelch their tendency to be emotional, impulsive, and quick-tempered. At their best, nines are highly evolved caregivers who endeavor to brighten the lives of those around them and to leave the world a better place than they found it.

BIRTHDATE: Those born on the 9th, 18th, or 27th of the month are nines. They're artistic, self-confident, take-charge individuals who need to feel that they're in control of their life and their future. Nines are determined to succeed, and they often have to fight for what they want, but make no mistake: They're formidable opponents when challenged. Nines are also generous, loving, and empathetic; they're born leaders who can easily inspire others to follow their good example. They need to feel needed, and they gravitate toward jobs and relationships that allow them to help other people or to fight for a worthy cause. If they want to evolve personally, it's important for nines to learn to move on when they outgrow a particular situation or partnership; clinging to the past will just cause them pain.

ELEVEN

DESTINY NUMBER: A Destiny Number of eleven is indicative of a higher calling in life. These idealistic individuals must strive to be humble and to cultivate their intellectual and spiritual knowledge. They're inspirational folks who thrive in the spotlight, and they're driven by the desire to uplift and serve their fellow human beings. The only caveat is that they have to guard against being too self-absorbed. Fully developed elevens are leaders of the highest order: evangelists, philosophers, entertainers, and teachers who were born to do good and to enlighten lesser mortals.

BIRTHDATE:
See **TWO**.

TWENTY-TWO

DESTINY NUMBER: A person with a Destiny Number of twenty-two has a destiny similar to that of elevens. Twenty-twos' purpose in life is to use their visionary, influential, humanitarian qualities to improve the world around them. Twenty-twos are natural diplomats who excel at bringing people together to work for the common good. They are highly motivated and quite disciplined when working toward a goal, and they're able to bring out the best in others, as well. They possess boundless physical and emotional energy, and are well suited to careers as teachers, politicians, or writers. Destiny Number Twenty-two offers an unprecedented opportunity to have a positive and lasting influence on the world.

BIRTHDATE: See **FOUR**.

PERSONAL YEAR,
MONTH, AND DAY NUMBERS

In addition to using numerology to analyze and better understand your personality, destiny, and unique characteristics, you can also use it to plan future events. The Personal Year, Month, and Day Numbers can help you determine the best time to undertake new projects or form new partnerships. These numbers provide information that enables you to make the most of any given situation.

You'll first need to figure out your Personal Year Number. This number provides insightful information about the twelve-month period in question. To do this, add your birth month and day to the current year, and keep reducing it until you have a single-digit number (except in the case of the Master Numbers of 11 and 22). Someone born on July 13th would add this

date to the current year, 1996, for example. So your personal year would be 9 (7 + 1 + 3 + 1 + 9 + 9 + 6 = 36, and 3 + 6 = 9).

The Personal Month Number is then calculated by adding your Personal Year Number to the current month. So, if you were born on July 13th and wanted to find out what to expect in June 1996, you would add your Personal 1996 Year Number (9) to the calendar month (6), for a total of 15, which is further reduced to result in Personal Month Number 6 (1 + 5). To look ahead to October of that year, you would again add your Personal Year Number (9) to that calendar month (10), for a total of 19, which reduces to 10, which is reduced even further (1 + 0) to Personal Month Number 1.

Your Personal Day Number narrows things down even more by letting you know what's going to happen on any given day.

This number is found by adding the current month and day numbers to your Personal Year Number. If our July 13th example wanted to know what to expect on, say, April 1st, 1996, they would add their current Personal Year Number (9) to the month and day, to arrive at a total of 14 (4 + 1 + 9 = 14), which reduces further (1 + 4) to Personal Day Number 5. Once you've calculated your Personal Year, Month, and Day numbers, read on to learn what the future holds (the indications for the Personal Year and Personal Month Numbers are the same).

ONE

Key Words: Independence, Beginnings, New Opportunities.

PERSONAL YEAR/MONTH: This is a period of fresh starts and new beginnings.

Strike out on your own and don't be afraid to take risks. If you're thinking of starting a new business, moving to a new home, or entering into a new relationship, there's no better time to put your plans into action. Your leadership potential is enhanced right now, so take charge and use it to your advantage. Whatever you begin during this period will need time to grow and flourish, so don't expect miracles. You are laying the groundwork and planting the seeds for future success, and it all hinges on your ability to be self-reliant and independent. A Number One Cycle is the perfect time to travel to unknown destinations, make career changes, establish new partnerships, and embark on new adventures of every kind!

PERSONAL DAY: It's a great day to begin new ventures, both personally and profes-

sionally. If there's a decision to be made, make it with confidence. Success will come easily today. Do something different.

TWO

Key Words: Patience, Teamwork, Companionship.

PERSONAL YEAR/MONTH: This is a time that requires cooperation, diplomacy, and, above all, patience. Career advancement, relationships—even life itself—are progressing at a snail's pace, but your best bet is to sit back, watch, and wait it out. Pay attention to what's going on around you. Change will come slowly during this period, but it's definitely on the way. Don't try to force the issue. When dealing with others, be support-

ive, understanding, and tactful. Your connections with friends and loved ones are very important right now; these relationships feed your soul and help you realize what life's all about. Use this quiet time to get some much-needed rest and to recharge your batteries. A Number Two Cycle provides an ideal opportunity for meaningful introspection and contemplation. Take time to reflect on where you've been, where you're headed, and what it is that you want out of life. Trust your instincts, and listen to your intuition.

PERSONAL DAY: This is the perfect time to make long-term plans or to complete niggling tasks that you've been putting off. Be kind and considerate toward other people, and let things

roll off your back.
Take it slow
today.

THREE

Key Words: Enjoyment, Imagination, Communication.

PERSONAL YEAR/MONTH: This is a

time to enhance your self-fulfillment by taking a more positive approach to life. Creative thinking is at an all-time high, so use it to solve a pressing problem or to figure out how to make yourself happier! Use your imagination to help further your career and make new contacts. You're feeling especially nurturing right now—don't be afraid to shower others with love and affection (you'll be amazed at the results). Concentrate on living life to its fullest and having fun. Redecorate your home or have a head-to-toe makeover. This is a great time to entertain and be entertained. Throw a party, take a vacation, go out with friends, and flirt like mad. You're feeling creative, lighthearted, expressive, and extremely sociable—revel in it. A Number Three Cycle is a time of great joy and harmony. Make the most of it.

PERSONAL DAY: This is an especially innovative, upbeat, and productive time. Today is ideal for brainstorming and creative problem-solving. Maintain a positive, cheerful outlook and you'll accomplish anything.

FOUR

Key Words: Organization, Practicality, Work.

PERSONAL YEAR/MONTH: This is a satisfying period characterized by planning, hard work, and determination

in both your personal and professional life. Productivity and perseverance are imperative right now; this is definitely not the time to be disorganized or to slack off. It is, however, the time to strengthen and build upon the foundation you laid in the Number One Cycle. Don't be afraid to roll up your sleeves and get your hands dirty—remember, whatever you invest in time and sweat equity now will come back to you tenfold. Your potential and willpower are unlimited during this period, so put them to good use. This is not to say that you should run yourself into the ground, however. If you feel physically exhausted or emotionally overwhelmed, take some time to unwind and renew your resources. The Number Four Cycle provides a unique opportunity for professional growth and personal self-improvement through diligent and persistent effort.

PERSONAL DAY: Today is the perfect time to fulfill professional obligations and to catch up on personal chores. Be methodical and persevere. Get up early, get organized, and do what it takes to get the job done!

FIVE

Key Words: Freedom, Change, Adventure.

PERSONAL YEAR/MONTH: This is a fortuitous period marked by tremendous growth and enormous, life-affirming change. It's an active, expansive, stimulating time, and you should take full advantage of your burgeoning lust for adventure and freedom. If you've always wanted to trek the Himalayas or scale Mount Everest, now's the time. Likewise, if you've been yearning to move to a distant city or make a drastic career change, go ahead and make the leap. The spotlight has been turned in your direction, and baby, you shine! Utilize this new-found popularity to advance your career or personal interests, but don't take on any long-term responsibilities (this is a time for spontaneity, not practical decision-making). You may be given a second chance at something you passed up a while ago; don't let this opportunity slip through your fingers. Your senses are working overtime now and you're completely in tune with everything that's going on around you. In fact, you feel at one with the universe, and you may feel compelled to work for the greater good (good for you!). This sensory overload also extends to your romantic relationships, and you may find yourself highly attracted to—and attractive to—other people (sex appeal, thy number is five). The Number Five Cycle gives you the chance to take risks, bend the rules, and test the limits you've set for yourself. By fearlessly embracing the challenges and surprises of this cycle, you'll reach new heights of self-discovery.

PERSONAL DAY: Dare to be different today. Don't shy away from new experiences or unusual situations. You'll enjoy yourself more if you maintain a flexible, open-minded attitude. If life throws you a curve ball, catch it and laugh. Score one for Spontaneity!

SIX

Key Words: Responsibility, Nurturing, Domesticity.

PERSONAL YEAR/MONTH: Now is

the time to focus on community, home, and family responsibilities. This is a period of outer-directed action and involvement; you should put your own concerns on the back burner for now and focus on the needs of other people. You're in a unique position to be of service and to promote good causes, and you'll get great emotional and personal satisfaction from doing so. This is also the best time to establish long-lasting friendships and cement personal relationships (in fact, the Number Six Personal Year is often called "the year of marriage"). Indulge your nesting instincts by redecorating your current home or by moving into a new one. Entertain at home and surround yourself with loved ones; you're in the mood to play

Mother Hen, so why fight the urge? The
more you give right now, the more you'll
receive in return. You may feel a bit put
upon at times, but selflessness is the key to
success during this cycle. Strive to be fair,
tolerant, and conscientious in your dealings
with others. The Number Six Personal

Cycle offers you an opportunity to enrich your own life by enriching the lives of others. You'll do well by doing good.

PERSONAL

DAY: It's an extremely sociable day, and you're feeling empathetic and receptive

48

toward other people. Make yourself available to friends and family, and offer help where it's needed. This is not the time for experimentation; stick to the tried and true.

SEVEN

Key Words: Introspection, Faith, Self-Awareness.

PERSONAL YEAR/ MONTH: This is a period of reflection and self-discovery. The more time you spend alone, the better. Use this opportunity to engage in the type of solitary self-analysis that inspires inner growth and personal knowledge: Meditate, embrace your spirituality, nurture your philosophical tendencies. Take the kind of solo trip—be it to Europe, Tibet, or a cabin in the woods—that promotes self-reliance and heightens self-awareness. Ponder the

meaning of life. Read weighty intellectual tomes that encourage self-examination and deep thought. But whatever you do, do it for *you*. This isn't the time to concentrate on business dealings, financial matters, or other people. In fact, it may be a good time to take a sabbatical from work or leave an unsatisfying relationship. Focus instead on yourself and your own dreams, desires, and personal development. This is a rather slow-moving period, and you need to maintain a calm, serene, patient attitude. If you try to manipulate the situation or to force change of any kind, you'll just feel frustrated and undermine your emotional well-being. The Number Seven Cycle gives you a chance to take stock of your life—past, present, and future. Use this interval to sort out your priorities and put things in order. Nurture your soul.

PERSONAL DAY: Spend time alone today, if at all possible. Read, take a long walk, and quietly contemplate the meaning of life. It's a good time to engage in spiritual, philosophical, and scientific ruminations. Self-examination is the order of the day.

EIGHT

Key Words: Achievement, Power, Recognition.

PERSONAL YEAR/MONTH: This is a time of unmitigated success and productivity. Self-discipline is key right now. If you stay focused and don't get lazy, you'll see tangible results of past efforts during this period—all your hard work finally pays off (and pays off big). Your self-confidence soars as a result, and you can wheel and deal to your heart's content. If there's something you want, now's the time to go after it—and don't be afraid to aim high, since your reach easily exceeds your grasp. Expect a blast from the past: You may have to repay an old debt (financial or otherwise), or renew contact with a long-lost friend or relative. Behave in an efficient, honorable, businesslike manner and big gains—professional, personal, and financial—will follow. Your belief in fate or destiny may be strengthened during this period. If you're involved in a serious relationship, this is a good time to make it official (or to declare your feelings and acknowledge your commitment to each other). A Number Eight Cycle provides an opportunity to achieve unheralded material gains, and personal and professional fulfillment of the highest order.

PERSONAL DAY: This is a good day to finalize plans, especially those related to business or financial matters. If you're feeling ambitious and the time is right, why not ask for that raise or promotion? (You *know* you deserve it—just be sure to dress the part.) Success is a sure thing today, as long as you maintain your dignity, composure, and integrity.

NINE

Key Words: Completion, Inspiration, Fulfillment.

PERSONAL YEAR/MONTH: This is a time of closure and conclusion, a time to let go of unfulfilling habits, relationships, and enterprises. By getting rid of these negative influences, you make room for positive forces to enter your life (hanging on to things you've outgrown will only weigh you down). If it isn't beneficial or uplifting in some way, out it goes! Review past accomplishments and begin laying plans for the future, but don't move ahead just yet. This is a time of resolution and renewal, not a time of action (this is true of matters of the heart, as well, so schedule first dates for another time). Be patient. Nurture your creativity, and work on improving existing relation-ships. Approach other people with an open heart and mind. Lend your support to a friend in need, and don't be afraid to ask for help from those in a position to give it. Compassion, cooperation, and forgiveness will go a long way toward improving the current state of affairs. Travel is especially advantageous during this period, as it can teach you more about yourself and other people (and there may be some lessons you need to learn in this area). The Number Nine Cycle is an inspirational period that affords you the chance to realize your dreams and to put old problems or unsatisfying situations to rest once and for all. Out with the old, in with the new!

PERSONAL DAY: This is not the time to begin anything new. Complete projects, fulfill obligations, and tie up any and all loose ends today (*gently*). It's the perfect time to clean out your closets or get rid of something you no longer have any use for (like that unsatisfying relationship). Indulge your humanitarian side by helping out someone less fortunate than yourself.

ELEVEN

Key Words: Intuition, Revelation, Idealism.

PERSONAL YEAR/MONTH: This is a once-in-a-lifetime moment (well, *almost*, anyway), during which all things spiritual and metaphysical are highlighted. You have a distinct sense of purpose now, and feel compelled to be of service to others and to work for the common good of your fellow Homo sapiens.

Go for it. You're also feeling especially inspired and creative when it comes to generating new ideas or solving problems, and you should use this talent to further your goals. Work on enhancing your peace of mind and emotional well-being. Treat others with kindness and compassion. If you ignore their flaws and applaud their strengths, they'll return the favor. This is a time for reflection and personal growth based on spiritual and intellectual enlightenment. You're in the mood for soul food (metaphorically speaking); seek and ye shall find. The Number Eleven Cycle is a special time in which you can achieve an unparalleled sense of personal illumination, spiritual fulfillment, and emotional contentment.

PERSONAL DAY: Forget about mundane concerns today. Instead, focus on the spiritual and intuitive side of yourself and the world around you. Take what comes, and let trouble roll off your back. Listen to your heart, not your head. Rise above petty grievances and set an example for others to follow.

TWENTY-TWO

Key Words: Greatness, Power, Achievement.

PERSONAL YEAR/ MONTH: This is a very rare period of supreme accomplishment and exceptional opportunity. Use this time to put your plans into action and to lay the foundation for future goals. Whatever you begin now is guaranteed to succeed. In fact, any project you undertake during this period will probably far surpass your wildest expectations, especially if it's global in nature or has far-reaching, positive implications. The bigger the plans, the bigger the payoff. By entering this cycle, you are being given the opportunity to have a long-lasting, powerful impact on the world at large. Don't pass it up (and don't mess it up by pandering to immoral or inferior instincts—yours or anyone else's). The Number Twenty-two Cycle presents you with a once-in-a-lifetime chance to leave the world a better place than you found it.

PERSONAL DAY: This is a day to put your own needs aside and to concentrate on helping others. Embrace your altruistic tendencies. You can achieve great things (including personal satisfaction) if you work for the greater good.